corpse whale

corpse whale

dg nanouk okpik

Foreword by Arthur Sze

THE UNIVERSITY OF
ARIZONA PRESS

TUCSON

THE UNIVERSITY OF
ARIZONA PRESS

© 2012 dg nanouk okpik

www.uapress.arizona.edu

Library of Congress Cataloging-in-Publication Data
Okpik, Dg Nanouk.
 Corpse whale / Dg Nanouk Okpik ; foreword by Arthur Sze.
   p. cm. — (Sun tracks: an American Indian literary series ; v. 73)
 ISBN 978-0-8165-2674-1 (pbk. : alk. paper)
 I. Title.
 PS3615.K75C67 2012
 811'.6–dc23
                    2012014966

Publication of this book is made possible in part by the proceeds of a permanent endowment created with the assistance of a Challenge Grant from the National Endowment for the Humanities, a federal agency.

Manufactured in the United States of America on acid-free, archival-quality paper containing a minimum of 30% post-consumer waste and processed chlorine free.

17   16   15   14   13   12   6   5   4   3   2   1

contents

foreword

dg nanouk okpik is Inupiaq, Inuit, and was raised by an Irish and German family in Anchorage, Alaska. Her family had ocean-faring boats, and, growing up, she fished in many rivers, lakes, and seaports. As a poet, dg okpik draws on her Inupiat heritage, but she is firmly rooted in the complexities, tensions, and challenges of our contemporary world.

In okpik's poetry, we often discover we are experiencing the world through contrasting mythic elements—"This day is made of horned puffins and Eskimo soothsayers"—and our experience of time moves from linear to synchronous. Past, future, and present co-exist, and this underlying conception of time strengthens the mythical elements in her work. The speaker of her poems is frequently locating and orienting: "marking   the direction south / on a walrus hide   of light-shadow   as if for / a fossil record."

The idea of a poem as a "fossil record" is an intriguing one, but mere retrieval from the past is insufficient to fulfill the visionary quest of the speaker. The speaker searches for something ancient yet contemporary, to find, in Wallace Stevens's words, "what will suffice." Here the words "as if" qualify the possibility of a poem as a fossil record: the poem may resemble a fossil record, but, instead of merely recording, the poem enacts a record of consciousness that leads to revelation. In section 3 of her marvelous sequence, "For the Spirits-Who-Have-Not-Yet-Rounded-the-Bend," the poem enacts, through memory, a vision of salmon moving upstream in cosmological light:

> I remember cleaning smeared smelt off my hooks sharpening them to catch
> mirror-back salmon, its fins spread, heading the opposite way, nosing up the
> river to spawn in eclipse water when the sun moves around the earth and all
> days are ebony backward.

dg okpik is always in pursuit of origins, but she writes an earth-centered poetry with urgency and with a flair for conflating the natural world with the mythic world of creation.

—ARTHUR SZE

Note: An earlier version of this introduction appeared in *American Poet: The Journal of the Academy of American Poets* 37 (Fall 2009).

corpse whale

In the time of origin, in the formation of *inuk*, she/I watch/es while the living awaits relatives to come from around the bend. Stoned to death, but not idle since the last ice age, Inupiat, by slow pounding and grinding, like a poultice in a mortar and pestle bowl devour *Kabloona* souls. Eustacy: She/I watch/es my *inua* fly out the sealskin porthole as smoke, as her/my ghost. She/I write/s these stories in a box. Buster Kailek, a Nunavut man once said, "The greatest peril of life lies in the fact human food consists entirely of souls."

—Pudlo Pudlat, Inuit Elder (1916–1992),
Cape Dorset, Hood Art Museum

Songs are thoughts, sung out with the breath when people are moved by great forces and ordinary speech no longer suffices. Man is moved just like the ice floe sailing here and there in the current. His thoughts are driven by the flowing force when he feels joy, when he feels fear, when he feels sorrow. Thoughts can wash over him like a flood, making his breath come in gasps and his heart throb. Something like abatement in the weather will keep him thawed up. And then it will happen that we, who always think we are small, will feel still smaller. And we will fear to use words. But it will happen that the words we need will come themselves. When the words we want to use shoot up of themselves— we get a new song.

—ORPINGALIK, shaman in Knud Rasmussen's Fifth Thule Expedition

in Pelly Bay, Canada

Earth = Mother = Adopted = Blood =
Raven in the midnight sun
Siqinq: Sun January
Siqinyasaq tatqiq: Moon of the coming
Sun *Itqaaq*: to recall and re-tell events
from long ago when cormorants flew on
the ice surfaces of sand blown landed
on points in a sound wave bearing a
peninsula. Mother, know she is/I am here
inside—just as your liver, as the coming
sun, or cold stark snow or when you touch me
briefly after birth. Eighty-four dark days of midnight
sun as the shadows of coastal ice caves,
nanoseconds of gravitational pull, above
clouds cache. Sixteen years later, she/is I/
am here cutting her/my thighs, bloodletting
in the mirror, praying to raven for light.

I.

Ceprano Man
900,000 years ago
        fled madly

toward the hills
        on foot
like a phantom

how do you tell
if weeks
        or moments go by
in the beginning
not seeing
but knowing

the rocks like words
        a millennium
of chalk marks and light
on the inside

image and art
like dusk
        on the outer-skin

of a cave like a flick or flint
        scratch on the stone of man

someone here
 there
roaming the rim
the gilded sun of home

a thawing ice house
        the raven's nest
        flaming whale ribs
saber-tooth tigers
eyeteeth incised
        petrified yellow forests

II.

Wolves and hyenas—after
        crushing bones
flavor-suck
        the marrow
        of their prey
they like to inhale
        the egg yolk
leave fragments
of skeletons

and rough skulls
eyeless   panting

        ggrr growling gggrrr

canines know when
you keep
        tripping
        at your weakest
fumbling on those
robust bones
        which
        keep laughing
those bones old—bones

        of Ceprano clacking
        at the center
of earth and
        echoing the hills.

III.

A fiend dog squints
            his incisors
just far enough

                                    away
to create space
            between us

looking for pieces

                        of pumice
to rub out the phlegm
            to throw lightly
                        on the wind

It's surprising
how much
                        you feel
when you find a skull
                        cap of an infant
in the desert
            on taiga

as if roaming   roaming

with distemper in Kamina-Zaire
or Kivalina-Alyeska

            hear them laughing

those bones   bones

a baby's brain capacity

seething as you
        hold it in
your hands like a fossil

finger the ridge of its brow.
Does it feel warm like mine?

IV.

Wolves and Hyenas

like   stalking stalking
their pride on light

padded-paws

they hunt together

       like uncles and cousins

in an *umiak* skin boat

or like brothers
         with black feet
on a lion sand   savannah
    or in a dust devil   dancing

waiting for breath bubbles

     to surface suspecting
a clutch around the neck

dragging across grit   snow
    with hounding
blood teeth

like a harpoon
     striking a place

of pulse a blowhole

or a long limber tail

with raised

haunches in *mukluks*
      in Africa our old home

or with bare-feet fleeing to Alaska
our new boreal forest.

Izrasugruk Tatqiq: February
Coldest Moon: *Tatqiq Kusruqaqtubvik*
Ice Moon Time Moon of a Higher Sun
Sauniq: Bones and moored pits of whale
blubber, hardy, sturdy, sod storehouses,
made from boorish ones, beat down adopted
sisters, brothers, cousins, and church.
It's a kept secret. Only in Raven's light
may we start. Inuit in bluffs and hills,
baleen gravesites of caribou skin left
behind, molding as *myouwls* cinch the noose
around her/my parfleche new.

Imieauraq's Ceremony of the Dead

Imieauraq, the prowler shaman
      is encrusted
with thick   stone   ochre   powder

he paints protection
he sets   his willow stick
      with a snare

      his protruding abdomen
          deforms his back
             now hunched
    and bowlegged
    he walks
          his bones knock
    the red dust settles.

                  (Imieauraq sees his older brother
                  storykeeper of the hunt in his dreams)

He traps a squirrel *siksrik*
for roasting a dinner
    for the dead

over the fire
          on every flint head
he ties notches   a piece of lashing

which drags and drapes
      across *siksrik's/squirrel's* neck.

                Imieauraq removes
the meat from bone

                intuitively

carefully skillfully

not to snag   a vein *(if it bleeds he'll need to use yo-yo's*
                              as protection
for his bear clan, for his sister's death wish)

he marks a bear skull in white paint: earth=mother=adopted=blood=raven=midnight sun

In his small plywood cabin
                              on the north shore

he runs in place   a slow runner
the cold settles   in his bulb knees
(he remembers: ice forming on the lagoon
                              when his sister fell in the ice water dead)
            he scrapes the squirrel's
                              tiny body
            closes the eyes   combs
each frozen   blue gray hair   until it is thawed.

He sponges   with a piece of moss   across the flesh.
            Wiping

dead   he remembers: *digging older strata*
dead   *descending*   *probing eroding flesh beaches.*
        He finds: in a burial site   up heaving   digging removing   a way out

        the eldest inuk   farther inland   in a house pit

then on every ridge   yellowed bodies bones
        bodies   bones   rising.

He heard this is what happens: when the water thaws
                leavening   uprising.

On Kotzebue Sound
        he places his sister's *kamik* legs and marmot arms
                        head and feet
                        upon a stilted
        driftwood altar   her crown of fireweed
                (he sees her ghost rise)

Imieauraq lays   wolverine furs over

               the appendages   flanks

      slips on her feet

           new *kamik* boots   *(his captain, his Umiliak,*

    new soles for the journey   *bear clan leader)*

            around the cosmos she will spin.

On his sister's hands   he places

         a pair of caribou mittens

fur-side in

      not to offend the spirits.   Below he drops

gooseberries   bearberries   snowberries

      in a seal poke   mixing it with reindeer marrow

             moose meat

      for the burial meal.

At last   the ceremony ends   he sets off

      to his *ugruk* breathing hole net

      on her day   he will catch a young seal

         ending

the ceremony   he tends his muskrat barrel

        sharpens his black

jade whetstones   collects water

      in his seal flippers *(waits for raven to bring the light)*

used as blood bottles   for dipping   *(he waits for the earth to turn)*

       in a shrinking pool.

Addled

the crevasse   of my waterlogged ear

damaged sound mixes as a hexed voice spreads   spreads

you bite into her/my scalp   down to the gray

one mistake

                   she/I listened to you   paid attention to

muddle   heard   heard

      how life on a rock causes the sun to be low

      how the stars are no longer seen

where   everyplace   they used to be

              used to be

                 to just be to exist   a living thing

look at the convulsions in the ocean   steel-engines

there   her/my breastbone snaps   snaps   rings

allowing my chambers to fill with blood   crushes down

like compressed throats   striking air   litmus red

I stomach both lungs   drowning in skin

stippled with dots short staggered line above lines

an old tattoo on my chin fading   fading   disappearing slowly
the period between   two thuds   thuds

          two contractions   one long delayed breath
                                        four minutes short of a solar day

my windpipe constricted   like a slender

stalk of rhubarb   sharp tasting   tight cords of time

          a pungent   rain silhouetted her/my

sharp bony cheeks before her/my   *kamiks*

hit   the   ground   patpatpatpat
bound by snow lilies   and arctic hares

a winch reels   in thought   of tinkered   eternity

and a whale   losing her   long-haired cheese clothed

piece of baleen   floats   smelled faintly   floats
ashore on Crow Island

in the rock niches around those subtle

          thoughts of dropping the   star

          and slicing   the blubber
of the belly   a gut rope of   death

a hundred and two times   over

a blow hole   slicing down

     to the distinct tale as sea nymphs

          wait for the parka

death feels like his enormous   blue baleen jawbone

    let me free to the krill and brine to
eat the mites

        lice and sea spiders

    she and I carry bird darts   for the future stalk of okpik

Paniqsiqsiivik: March
March moon: She is/I am hanging seal
and bleaching caribou skins
Ugruk: spotted seal lying in a pile:
ivory labrets in cheeks with tattooed
chins rising in rifts of stout rock,
sponge lichen, carved dishes tarsal pipes,
my mummified face with a bone nose ring
ribbon seal bags sewn from flipper to flipper,
like my arms stitched with silk twine she/I
carry/ies bird darts for the future stalk of *ukpik*.

Moon of the Returning Sun

A view from two sides of Polaris, it is said:
> the living awaits destined relatives to retort.

These people go around waking the sleeping ones
when the weather is good: *they wait for those*
> *who-are-coming-around-the-bend.*

1981 *Anaktuvik* Pass/*Tulugaq* Elijah *Kakinya* Inupiaq name *Kainnaaq* said,

> *"In the beginning of the universe,*
> *when you were young long ago,*
> *the sky was dark and underneath us.*
> *Down under there was no sun until*
> *the world turned over and became*
> *the sky we have now."*

> It is said: Down under lived two wolves
> who had two children, a boy and a girl.

From these wolves-of-part-man, all the people
> came to be and multiplied.

I as wolf girl   became weary of the light
dwell in darkness   long time ago I was taken
away from *Utqiagvik*   by the ones in black cloaks,
> adopted.

I wait for the universe to turn

> around again,

> wait for a reason to move the fetus in my womb
> wait for Raven to bring back the sun
> for   recovery/extraction

> with a sealskin satchel
> birch bark and pencil
> wolf girl rewrites tundra.

Riding *Samna*'s Gyrfalcon

She/I dream/s in flight with falcon.
                    She/I glide/s in an Inuit ice shelf

through cobalt haze,
          then down to the beluga's tail.

Over glacier   salmon-pink spires,
        she/I feel/s old and young
                    both like a lost
mother or found   earth   girl child
            salvaged
        chasing tracks of aged caribou
                  and avalanche rivers.

Gyre Falcon and she/I dip/s
            across muskeg down

to tundra spruced flowers;
        the ice is cracked-blazon
                cranberry and air hardy.

Her/my songs call shadows
                to lie sideways
and shamans to sway
           in the northern tilt
              of ten thousand years of ease.

Alders twitch
        from gales of bellow-winded ice spray,
                still granite   quiet statues
           chilled to night   in the obsidian burrow.

The gemstone frost   on driftwood

          alongside brooks,
coiling   recoiling,
          mixing with my   scattered drum strikes.

Nesting cubic dust and chert whittled in soapstone,
          my throat songs
vibrate
vibrate   into migrations of flames.
vibrate
Famine reaches the stalked   earlier than the stalker.
To *Sila*:

the she/I use/s a mace adze on nightmares

hatchet a carving on soapstone for a face

in three stages
                              up shore
remote villages   sink

she/I wander/s in from the outside one of those with hair for skin
she/I count/s bowhead in magnetic storms

thunder claps the tree branches in the wind
Sila uses open water currents

                        to pinpoint

the degree north inside.   *Sila* brings light and taut

willow roots for fire starting.

She/I say/s: Bear grease brings warmth. The stink

unbearable

we tend to our hair and flesh, so we don't fade

in the low land shapes of ghost. They trick us with faint

amperes, pantomimes. We use this leaf for a cup

       to drink the 29 degree rain.

Somewhere an *inuk* with a broad nose inside me

falls to her knees,   a Dall sheep bites into her/my scalp
into the jellied brain   she/I swagger/s outside reaching her/my limit

drinks the cold sheep's milk a substitute for alcohol.

Mask of Dance

A wooden face is carving

the *inua* inside a bird beak.

Nearby heads open the lighted

crawl spaces of knotted plumage.

Gauze rings of dog moon,

leashes to lifelines, sway from dwellings.

Bentwood quill eyes

or half circles, not finished, like divided hoops.

Threaded strings dangle

tilted soapstone heads tied from wrists

the face twists and distorts her muscles.

The being awakens with quaking

fingers of death, snatches—

life is not a rock of hollow thorn.

Paint with brushes an amulet shield.

Wear soot and ashes,

with the red dial inward,

clock attachments outward.

Trace the day of charred white spruce,

rimmed in hands, with no thumbs.

Storyteller in the yellowed

mind of matter,   halt and pivot.

A wingless and anchored battle,

a gloved white patch of epidermis;

under the breast, inside which,

hatching snowy owls

claw and peck the pink shells.

Bluebird's song from the spotted mantle

in motion scats on air-drums.

The palm dancers return,

with sleight-of-hand tricks

flashing over the burn pile.

The other mask surfaces

then transforms into seal whiskers.

Agaviksiuvika Tatqiq: April
Moon for beginning whaling
and finding ptarmigan
aarnaruie suliuqpa: Savannah
sparrow she/I use/s jagged
sea strokes with paddles
on glass, her/my Eskimo
goggles of life seek giant
whale people. In land flint
spears the motherland. She/I
slice/s our fingertips with
obsidian to erase prints.
A savannah sparrow falls into
a mirror of ice melting, the
brown perma-slick in turn
gives birth to Eskimo, a blood
Snow Bunting, and kittiwake.

The Fate of Inupiaq-like Kingfisher

But no one can
stop
a bird spear set
in motion,

made of notched bone,

feathered arrows pinnate

around the shaft,

with hair fringe
as it strikes

piercing depilated skin.

Some humans weave themselves

with lime grass,
into large orbs.

Others make goosefeet baskets

of seaweed or with narrow leaves,

or collect matches or tobacco.

The lamp soot burns like gas.

On Clovis point a circular icy reef,

my existence becoming a flicker

like the orange scales of a kingfisher.

We pirouette, diving, diving,

                                   deep.

Drying Magma Near Illiamna

We lying in the onyx rain   by garnet-cloaking icebergs.

We watch   on jet spires polar bears
  hunting   snowdrift   urchin of Inuit

then edged puffin   on bluffs with nests

filled with ruby   eggs of egrets.

In moss   picking gooseberries,
wearing   wrinkled skins of ivory   and lichen
where boar tides swirl   haywire Inupiat

they said, the men in black cloaks will mutilate our known selves

shocked   with eel   swim as their teeth grind.

Our bull walrus   amulets   snort and turn placid
as our screams
       of lightning pass. Our slanted eyes

    lurk and twitch   blood gales.

We clad the night   with dead polar bears

stuck on ice.   Bears and seas

    abide in a salt prison.

Trails of sea cows   reach the mountains

                with meltwater   draining off the peaks.
As we cast   solar rays   to cliffs   our seal

oil lamps flicker   and our igloos   glow.
In night   we rest by brooks of amphipods
spawning net stories   feed on bloated
intestines   of full
                              robins with bellies of globed eggs.

We live in earth mounds   along the Norton
Sound   which mutate   into slat board
quiver into the sea
Alyeska   liquefied by heat dissolves into mud.

Flats   where steam rises to ashes   lava rock

            float in ten thousand   smoke rings smoke

rings of fire opal panning phantoms of cod children.

Samna's craters   of solar dust collect sonic

whale songs.   Throat murmurs   of old
weathered ladies   wearing moose hides,
flowered scarves   walking   rocking

in a billowed gait   like bold Bering mastodons

galloping across   Skeleton Butte   as bone mares.
Galloping

Squawking silence   permeates the white
volcanoes   where ancestors dance \ light candles
in redux furs   fins   and black raven feathers.

            Golden eyes of
                  Polaris with his seven adopted sisters
pack ice melt.   Musk oxen can't guard nuclear
grasslands   from brown air   thin water.

The sea salt burns blisters   into sores
while the whale ribs split   fissure

as *Samna*'s right   hand remains clenched
during the spring thaw.   In five minutes
a mosquito sucks
                juice from a Fulmar's vein, then from kids' forearms

women shape   cinder cones while tying
willow-gray   braided hair,   aging the sisters
twelve thousand years young.   Serpentine
women touch minerals   of DNA to gather strength
shark teeth   necklaces lure   cairn rock   prayer from sulfur
        and demon flowers.

Days of Next Yesterday

When she/I feel/s the weight   of plastered walls,
brick doors closing heavy

                windows slamming
she/I like/s to crawl into an igloo   chute tunnel to the center
of snow   strip down to her/my inner clothes

 fur-side in.   She/I peel/s away the marmot skin
        smell a pot of Labrador   tea boiling.
In her/my plank grave   she/I lay/s under sod
my teeth gnaw
        on dried herring,   eider eggs, sip tea.

With a whale oil lamp lit   she/I watch/es *Aapaga grandfather*
melt snow for water.   Watch the ice shrink.
No polar bear in days.

Aanaga grandmother   sews the worn heels of *aapiyaba brother's kamiks.*
No blue snow   only white rain.

She/I watch/es them   lift the toils   of burdened life   a steel-head
plague
plague
plague   as she/I shovel/s   in front of my feet
        throw peat moss   into a mammoth's mouth
with no roe   no narwhal   no reserves.

Suvluravik Tatqiq: May
Moon When the Rivers Flow
Spring: *Upinagasrak*
Thaw: *Sikuibvik*
Ptuquqsiibayuk: Stag Beetle
Qupixbubrauq: Edible Ice Worm
Moon when fawns are born,
like: returning eider ducks,
or her/my plasma made of
stag beetles lily flowers
in pearl wombs velvet wombs,
caribou horns, water ouzel
and radiocarbon dating
by imprint toggling.
Do you feel her in me
mother? We are one. These are
not peregrine falcon eggs
smeared on a microscope slide;
it is me/him as a creeper
or water worm sharpening
the ice core.

Stereoscope

Stereoscope:

                      A device by which two

photographs

                      of the same object takes

slightly

                      different angles are viewed

together

                      giving an impression of depth

slightly wide

                      as in ordinary human vision.

Even now   the pink eustachian tube
from the back   of my raw   pharynx
emits short   quick notes
          half-blood
the frequency   of my haddock song.

She/I cut   cut   cut   tear   cut   cut

patterns on my arms   inside the pits   below sock-line
to tell a story.   Just as chrysanthemum
      petals radiate   from   one orbit seed

you continue to unfold   infinitely

orb ladders   galaxies of jade   dimensions
      you sing and I   bleed out slowly
the deeper I cut
      around the same point,   point
curving at different   levels   where blue burning

changes to scald flesh   is not enough.

How is it you conjure   seabird specimens
from my skull   which collapses   inward,
when blood clots?
                    How do you mention
one by one   our place-names
and dates of birth   by labeling   your glass boxes?
How do you print   on heavy flat paper
the artifacts of *Nuiqsut*   which makes me
pull apart my cartilage?
          You see   she/I think/s
you would   like to extend the ghost surface

of this row   of death loops   and flatten
the blood bevel   between   two stopping
places because   notes squat and sprawl.
And you with the sidelong foul glance
become   whiter and ruffled   because

she/I came with my/our own things.   Upon arriving,
she/I spliced willow   connected it with seal twine
made laments.   She/I carved with hind molars what
she/I envisage/s   on her/my limbs   as   a tattoo   looking into your
deep eyes   with no shine   she/I saw roots lost in a dead walk.

Pearl Serpents in Trance

They wore amulets   of pearl for *Samna,*
some walked in seal form   also in ice bears

snow owls.   Flakes   forged the color   yellow
snow tigers   and fades   into the mountain ledge.

If you split elixir   from the green   and not know
Why   then we float   like sea spiders

      in the deep.   If you hex and confuse

      the ill form of a ten-legged   bear with a thousand toenails

  you smother Eskimo   children with no marrow
       or earthen ligaments.

The shape of man   is no longer   amber sap drying

on furrowed bark.   Man's pitch does not heal skin
any longer.   Do not dig up charred driftwood,   sedge
grass baskets   fossilized bones.   Use lineage
of *Uqaluktuat*

reach for reed pillars   of north Asia as
once
       when we hummed the same guttural song.

Palmed Hands Foist Dice

In *Kuukpik*   she/I become/s   aware of the evil
Spirits   let no one be in any doubt

of the remedies from *Anatkuq the magician*
for the white illness.   The *anatkuq* radiates fire.

In a cave he prepares the poultice in a mauve clay
bowl with cotton grass   seal liver cubed dice
                              rain water.

As if his palms   of ivory throw   rocks for a healing.
He tosses   dice in a game of probability
                                    in black peat soil.

She/I consider/s the patches   of seawater
where devils   clack and claw upward

toward   the sun surface.   She/I use/s old songs.

        Anatkuq's urchins   cross fishnets into gnarls
                    tie knots in a web.

Having found   blue demons in a sideslip
of grotto clouds   reflecting on the water

she/I remain/s   until the sky is gray   then assail the dice.
You see she's/I'm watching *Anatkuq's* reflection. She's/I've only played

this game   a couple of times.   She/I learn/s fast: survey
read, recite, review.   Again, again.   She/I pick/s up a feather

brush,   paint/s a sign   used in music thresholds:
extinction,   Algebra marking the direction south

on a walrus hide   of light-shadow as if for

a fossil record.   Only a few transcribe pictures

to words.   She/I came to the fire,   next to the snow cave
          lead pieces   to draw   on the seal hides

to take witness of *Anatkuq*'s   curing.
                 She/I   flint-spark/s   the stone
pumice burns, the song rises.   She/I memorize/s the puzzling words.

             OPEC,   *Yellow Sea China,*   *Chukchi,*
Gulf of Mexico,   *Beaufort Sea,*   *Niger Delta,*
Valdez,
      she/I call/s upon   the coldest moon to react to the equinox
the age of earth   already intact   she/I throw/s the *Anatkuq*'s ivory dice.

Ninilchik

Grandfather said: Drink the icy, glacier water.
Velvet sponges seep and hack disease, Ulu cuts.
We are rooted in landscapes our shares preserved,
oil peaking, and campgrounds full of tourists.

Eddie Baue had rising salmon.
Us, starfish red and razor clam fed.
Ninilchik sand bluffs with fire hot grit,
joining smoke mountains then, bailing.

Russian Orthodox cross, a double helix.
Gulch the pearls, choke on splinters of fireweed.
Black trees smoldered; dunes corral ice
in marsh gold amulets of ivory feathers.

Safety belts strangling, strangling
us with thick hair, braided black like petroleum.
Sienna sunsets, raining sinew
line the shell banks and twitch bone.

Ghosts of concrete sludge ready to pounce.
Then daily feed of twin rainbows rise above.
Volcanoes jetting behind the gray rock
pelicans wade in crests of bubbles.

Seaweed the length of trees, salty protein,
the sea rises to snatch the spotted seal
with sharp eyes, I watch the feathers
of plucked gulls, teeth gnarled and beaks pointed.

A pecking order in delicate alder nests,
my north wind punches, squalling rubber algae.
Jellyfish plunge into cement splashing,
offering pebbled soapstone and jade.

Japanese fishing floats shatter, hovering
water glass the color of Coke bottles.

Bess and Raven

Bess walks for long distances. *Agaayuvifmufniaqtufa (I'm on my way to church)*. On her way inland, she tells me of a raven who carries an Eskimo bone in his beak. *Afipchabaa (Resurrects him)*. Raven followed her up a switchback into alders where she built camp. *Nipiruq sunset* is late coming. Bessie knew about latecomers and bones. Born when the world was up-side-down, she likes to repent and turn over ash. In the beginning, she and Raven told stories from the old world, made a pact, and carved it on a soapstone tablet. Like a barbed bone harpoon or an *inuk*'s inherent capacity to kill a seal, the sun rises to the moon warm and blue. Bessie uncovers the capacity to manifest energy of Inupiat, plants, and animals.

Raven: *These travelers trade time and they never thought of ieuujiq life sliced separate from nature. They live with the caribou Botfly larva. It's a backward time: each second lasts for a Pula solar eclipse in June when the days shorten and like a trap: the metal snaps, the weight crushes the prey. How quickly it snaps. Snaps.*

Ibeivik: June Birth Time
When animals give birth
Upinagaq: Summer
Qusrimmak: Wild rhubarb
blueberries, salmonberries,
crowberries, fresh shoots
of fireweed to eat,
her/my nipples hard like hoary
marmot teeth, she/I smell/s
of stinkweed, willow leafs,
tree roots, hailstones.
It's her/my time to carve
oars to make her/my
umiak or *kayak* skin boat.

If Oil Is Drilled in Bristol Bay

for Sarah Palin

Why is it, in Bristol Bay, a sea cormorant
hovers, sings a two-fold song with a hinged cover

for a mouth, teeth set in sockets, with a hissing grind
of spikelets biting the air? Dip one.

The lips of vanished flames in lava coals
glow vermillion as an egg cracks. Dip two.

She/I feel/s a chimera leaving the eider duck. Dip three.
While still in the embryo, separating the body

from death she/I smell/s of arsenic, the Chugach Range
in unnatural bitterness. Why is it, man's/woman's nerve scarcely

stifled and sane, comes to prey? While they swoon
minerals of crude oil and sea spiders for tricking a way for gold.

Will they crawl around her/me, sink their eyeteeth in the sea,
ravaging the ecosphere and the ore gold for fuel. Drill.

No Fishing on the Point

Look at my/her engraved chin   made by deep lines of soot-ink.
        See the groove across her/my face.
A bull caribou   tramples my shoulders,   pins

her/me to the roof rock,   tethers my backstrap.   Boxed   in ice
cellars,   bowhead meat ferments,   freezes
to jam.

A shotgun blasts the sky to alert the plywood shacks
of migrating bowheads. The CB voice alerts: "*AAAIIGGIAARR*"
the house pits and Quonset huts which line the shore of ice laden waters, gray dorsal fins
rise on the Beaufort Sea. A chore-girl in rags, she/I sit/s lotus-legged, weaving baleen
baskets.

        Here, brother watches   and waits for
             the correct time   to strike,
right above the   blow hole.
        Here, it is a clean kill. Blood water all around us.
        Here, a woman far away crying for the whale's soul.

But, the men still heave to the beach

another day and a half. Pulling, winching,

pulling, dragging.

She/I cut/s opaque flesh and black meat with a jagged *ulu*,
carve *muktuk*, tie dark and white ribbons on each
gunnysack to mark the body parts. She/I slice/s the dorsal fin, give it to my brother
for ceremony, barter a bag of whalebones for fuel to heat the aged and chilled cement
barracks.

On *Birnirk* for thousands
of years called Point Barrow.
Now here,   a duck site a place of trade, where a DEW line
crosses
an old military port of call   for sighting air attacks,
where they want
to claim the sea for roads.   She's/I've watched the currents,
migrations, felt the rough movements
of the ice, which brings feasts, and famine.

Salt Cedar on Kokonee at Susitna River

but finding no resting place, returned; then I sent forth a raven.
The raven flew off, and seeing
that the waters decreased, {Cautiously} waded in the mud, but did not
return.

— *The Epic of Gilgamesh*

I.

When the mud dried, black spruce culled
at the river's lapse, I slouched over to fill my mouth—
the ice-packed gorge flowed over my fingers.
I cupped then drank. Right hand first, left followed.
Is this the way to the earth? I've stood still
but, the sea and sky kept circling, circling
the midnight sun. I did not return.

II.

In the loft, I found one carved wing of yellow cedar
resting at the bottom of the netted cage.
Foul and cold air swept by me. *Aaka* called,
I dropped the wooden wing, fled down the ladder
to a black bird in a mask. A box of suet spilled.
I ran to the river to meet the ocean's edge.
I returned at dusk.

III.

Ellipse of the moon when the sun is lowest—
harp, timpani, bass, viola, flute,
wavelengths of woodwinds.
The nimbus darkened, a gingko fan leaf
measured candela carbon in the expanse,
Genesis at dense blithe. The bell on the mountain
rang beyond the scape: echo, echo.

IV.
Blackfish parr, swimmer of freshwater—
urn of eggs pocketed in rocks,
swimmer flow past in this moon—
for you, brackish season's leap.
So it is, you breathe quantum lux
and return, return, and return.

Demons in a Quonset Hut

She/I feed/s demons,   louse eggs,   excrement,
and fresh   pussy willows.

She/I set/s traps   with Burbot bait. She/I play/s string games with *Tuungaq* the devil

to lure them out of the Quonset mimicking their coaxing black eyes, a sneered smile.

Squatting,   rubbing, and   twisting fire-grained driftwood,   trembling
she/I pound/s bone

in the shape of juggling stones.   She/I set/s the fire while twigs crack.

She/I feed/s the *Tuungaq*   small dried whitefish, rubbing with fish oil, grouse
eggs.

We leave the hut   go down   to the riverbed to
trapped grayling   in a fish basket.   As we enter

the cold, clear water   our feet turn cloven, our fingers curl,
toes forging together. They say: *She/I feed/s devil's beluga skin. She/I feed/s demons.*

 She/I butcher/s membranes down shore,   covering
her/my flesh,   her/my eyes,   with soft snow,   to
absorb the vivid bloodletting   for

a sacrifice to the god to forgive us.

Date: Post Glacial

A fern curls and drinks   water next   to the Chena River;
she/I engrave/s   with drill bows   the tattoos

        layered   on the backside of a gray whale,
polish   with cotton in circles   to bring out the design.

Over the sea black-whales   arch and span,
        while four-sided sabers   guard the processing

        barge—a city atop the sea.

Pollen lands   where the air is good.   Dig for chert bone.

Find an antler.   Reel in the velvet   make a map for trade.

 Small wooden faces   flat   with skin-lined splinters ask:
        Should we prune   *more trees or tag and replant?*
We   the Red Stone people
        keep our millwork central.
In the New Stone Age   don't let the paddlewheel rust.

Around our chins   tie the knitted   musk oxen hat
with ivory toggles   firm and fixed.

Kiln powder in beveled pools   on beetle rust greens.
        The talc settles   no rain in seventeen days.

Invent a fan to blow   the north wind   to cool the ivory bone etch.
The tall grass

calls bent birch   snowshoes to make tracks. *Do we run*

a tap dry of soot   *and sludge to forge roots?*

How many drink   wild tea, dip blubber in seal oil?
From the horizon   she/I watch/es fire opals   come from

molten rain,   the clay mass   returns to
                      full grass baskets.

Inyukuksaivik Tatqiq: July
Moon when birds raise their young
plump breasted snow geese swaddle papier
mâché eggs. Her/my mother's feather blanket
nestles an albino seal. Years ago, it could
have been her/me nestled safely in a snow cloth.
She/I wait/s for the next ten thousand years of
fossil replica, she/I wait/s until my adoption
has worn off her/my mind where pixels turn into
satellites and nightmares.

Little Brother and Serpent *Samna*

1.
She/I play/s in fields of tall grass and sticker bushes,
that snag on her/my *atiguluq* and white tights.

2.
Little brother skips between moose tracks
and chinked sod houses. She/I sing/s shrill echoes
of red snapper and razor clam shells underfoot.

3.
Blood leaches on her/my shins
collect in wading mosquito pools,
nettle days fester nightfall into salmon sky pink.

4.
Copper mountains and elderberries linger upon Knik Arm,
just between the knots on silver birch burnt spruce.

5.
Mount Williwaw and purple iris below white
Polaris star remind me nightly of youthful delight.

6.
Her/my tent bays on the shore of Cook Inlet,
next to the gulls and charred fir trees,
darkening the sun, cloud by cloud.

7.
Brother's crooked head atop mother's sucking barnacles,
hold him in bore tides of milky water.

8.

Fishing lines hook his sealskin *mukluks*,
feet cemented in rock base, gray quicksand,
he jigs blue hooligan off the point.

9.

Ash mother's mouth like Serpent *Samna* both with
a tendril grasp, tainting him raw sienna.

10.

The mother's milk my brother from each bosom.
He nibbles at his browbeating umbilical cord,
seeks a pacifier of Barter Island, seal sunning.

11.

Samna brings brother close enough to smell the blue ruin,
Yet far enough to build a castle made of tentacles.

12.

He plays tug-of-war and hopscotch with next of kin.
The seahorse saddled and bucking from the spurs
of brackish headwaters and iced shells of razor clams.

13.

She/I left a century ago beyond the castle
into the moat of beadwork; made a sand spit;
an island erected into my likeness: made of pigment,
ivory paper with black scrimshaw pictures.

Uqaqtaa
God Brings Her/Me to the Next Mind

a.

She/I prick/s my cheek with squid poison,
bone chisel a deer's scapula.
She is/I am an incised clay figure without meteor origin,
without a fire-stone end, she/I sit/s in the sill of the doorway,
which flexes half-open, half-closed.
She/I want/s any place of entering or leaving,
dark beyond deeper fevers. She/I remember/s,
shipworms eating out cellulose my antlers
like long mesh conduits coaxing my head.

b.

A black shaman excises her/my tongue
which smells of persimmon, hickory,
dark ring nuts. She/I sit/s like a bottom feeder
unmoved by the outside mind. Casting, spinning
my delusions which tap my thoughts
of limits, a place whereupon the *inua*
calls in red deer with teeth of a dog.

When Frog Songs Change

Is it in   this everlasting   murmur she/I walk/s?
Does life only come to the   alienated—

the ones   in diaspora   with no home,
                    so they escape   to TRON.
Her/my life-cord
craves color,   scent,   touch,   a deeper texture

            of the inside.   In a place   on the river-

banks of the Chena   she/I sit/s and erase/s
            the dense ash fall. Knowing she/I cannot   fill
with silt her/my carbon footprint   but she/I can
send to the seed vault   her/my fireweed,

cod eggs for Beluga,   copepods
for bowhead.   The first time   the seeds

were meant   for babes of the taiga.
But now   knowing the frog's mating

calls   have changed   due to bat predation
she/I horde/s splinters   of life fleeting   as in motion

measured by sensors   connected to dances
of pantomime   echo-collusion glancing

off surfaces of herself/myself   she/I step/s walk   into cyberspace.

Cell Block on Chena River

First: Brother, remove the tool marks on your scathed skin, brush your tattoos with
nettles, smear bearberry juice in the gashes. Crack open the jail-seed.

Second: Tear away the bars which restrain
your lean, spare life. Bend your curves in a knot. Brother, smudge your
saw-tooth edges.

Third: Cut red seaweed to conceal your gray cadaver;
start wetting your skin down; after scraping,
drip your bowels of blood, change into wolf.

Fourth: The savannah sparrow flies north.
In speech, smell fine-grained hawthorn.
Collapse your voice into bark and howl.

The Shaman Palpates Her/My Body with Voices

Surround me/her with fermented whales,

shaman holler and pound the bones on a drum.

The fat covered membrane like a crystal ball

reveals the willows feed off toxic sea berries,

reveals the crack in the ice for the hunters

to avoid the trapline.

The shamans use mortar-filled skin over the brain skull

to help drown their murmured voices. She/I lie/s awake.

And asleep, but jostled, she/I gouge/s tracks in the snow

like hind legs of caribou who thrust at the earth.

The shamans grind white fish liver into paste,

covering their foreheads to their chins. Start palpating.

They formed through the mouths spikes of cream

flowers, red roots sink and smear their hum.

They wrap cartilage around the jawbone like baleen,

so she/I might come to know our songs: pale to the grave.

Aqavirvik Tatqiq: August
Moon when the birds molt
Qurraquaraq: killdeer
A longspur arctic loon,
like a willow stump for
her/my arms, black guillemot,
speckled eider, 82 to 87
percent carbon by weight
12 to 15 percent hydrogen,
imagine a sandpiper of
paraffin (her/my mother says)
as she/I drift/s away
freely. Little brother
following as they all do.

~~Under Erasure~~ Beliefs and Values: INUPIAQATIGIIGNIQ: Using ~~tools~~ ~~ENGLISH words~~
in a new way ONE WORLD ~~NOT TWO~~ He said: *do you see the tree? She said: WHAT TREE?*
Spirituality: UKPIQQUTIQAGNIQ = Christianity = tradition = ORAL
MYTHS = bible = creation ~~PRIMITIVE = SAVAGE = PRIVILEDGED =~~
~~UNDERPRIVELDGED = CIVILIZED = uncivilized~~ Elders = Infants =
Children = Adults = Seniors = Elders = Ilagiigniq = family = kinship = roles
OTHERS = US = THEM = SHE = HE = ~~ANIMALS~~ = HUMANS = ROCK = ~~BIRDS~~ = WATER
= ~~FISH~~ SIGNATAINNIQ = Sharing = cooperation = love = respect = compassion = humility =
she = he = us PAAMINAAGIINNIQ = PIQPAKKUTIQAGNIQ = one another = NALIKKU
TIQAGNIQ = QINUINNIQ****** QINUINNIQ****** humility HUMILITY qinuinniq*****
*QINUINNIQ ~~Avoidance AVOIDANCE avoidance OF of CONFLICT conflict avoidance AV~~
~~OIDANCE~~ LAUGH giggle QUVIANGUNIQ jokes FUNNY teasing COUSIN just kidding
OUTROAR jolly UNDERERASURE ~~undererasure~~ UNDERERASURE ~~undererasure~~
UNDERERASURE UNDER under UNDER under UNDER under UNDER under UNDER
under UNDER under Erasure ERASURE erasure ERASURE erasure ERASURE erasure
ERASURE erasure ERASURE DEFER defer DIFFER defer DIFFER difference SAME same
ONE one ONE one WORLD world INUIT eskimo INUIT eskimo ESKIMO inuit ESKIMO
inuit greenlander INUKITUT inuk INUA inuk ~~anuniagniq ANUNIAGNIQ grocery store~~
~~MINUTEMART fastfood JUNKFOOD whale seal walrus masuru WILD CELERY wild~~
~~onion HAMBURGERS soda PEPSI/COKE water water water water glacier GLACIER water~~
~~BEAUFORT SEA bering sea OCEAN OCEAN OCEAN OCEAN OCEAN~~
language forms us, we exist, we think, we see, we feel, ENGLISH = INUPIAQ english
INUPIAQ (he said) (Derrida) (Jacques) the shape of a thing of a person, of a particular
mode character INTERNAL APPEARANCE = EXTERNAL   APPEARANCE and out =
life = US What is the sign? signified? signifier? image? word? conjure? stories? complex
experiences = INUIT sound image gesture pronounced verbalized said spoken RAISE YOUR
EYEBROWS if you know be bebebebebebebebebebebebbebee BE bebebebebebebebb BE bebe
bebjustbe JUST BE justbebebeba doption ADOPTION assimilation IDENTITY theft
HISTORICAL GRIEF healing HEALING ONE ONE ONE ONE ONE whole whole whole
not half not apple APPLE eskimo outside AT LARGE referrefer deferdeferereferdefer POST
PONED postponed PROLONGED tone voice speak spoken postponement of meaning
MEANING play of words PUN humor TRACE WORDS refer defer refer
he said: *Is she comparing the tree to herself? THE TREE IS BIG the tree is big OR is she merely*
informing us that the tree is big? How big? Compared to what other tree? Is it a GINGKO
or ALDER or DRIFTWOOD or A LIFE TREE the tree OR just a tree Or a cross or boat?
Imagined REALITY logic FEELING reason REAL fake HUMAN   we are only human
take pity Is it concept? Is is referential? Is it a seal oil lamp? Is it a twig? Is it a people called
Eskimo? REDISONLY RED BECAUSE WE AGREE IT IS RED or is it green? Or blue? How
is it the same? Borrow borrow borrow borrow borrow borrow borrow borrow borrow borrow
borrow borrow borrow TRANSFORM transform TRANSFORMATION transcend SHIFT
shaPE reincarnate CARNATE What would whale say? WHAT WOULD SEAL SAY? what
would inuk say? WHAT WOULD INUA? Ugruk? sila? SILA? Christ/God? WATER   SAYS
WHAT? HOW DOES WATER SOUND? How does water feel? How does it taste? Is it
ice! GLACIER? Is it Man? (98%) 2% what then? INUA? What do we understand of this
imagined tree? the trace words? WHAT DO THEY THINK OF US IF THEY BELIEVE
WE NEED SUCH INFORMATION? Is it an evergreen? Do we think we are just learning?
Are we adults? Are we whales? Are they trace words TRACE THE WORDS tracing forms
TRACE TRACE TRACE ERASE Erase UNDER above are we reliable? Is English a mold as
Inupiaq? WHAT IS THE CONFIGURATION? A+B+Ce=mc2 CONSTANT LIGHT
what is the relation between a black beetle and a black hole? / FLEA & TIME? ME YOU INUIT
ESKIMO white red brown yellow ADOPTED raised in the village TRADITIONAL modern
EDUCATED experienced SUBSISTENCE inupiaq ENGLISH inupiat INUKITUT kallit

The Pact with Samna

****

The ice chisel sculpted her Mother's Day.
Ash mother sent another caribou calf during
the first year, through the sprawling white marsh, scrambling
with pack and paddle, on hooves of driftwood.
****

She put on a carved mask with snowy owl feathers,
then, danced a long, limp, *mukluk* shuffle.
A clock struck the twenty-fourth hour, her life-line
was thirty-six years; she knew *Samna* would betray her.
****

The jawbone of *Birnirk* was the place to give her up,
clad in calico flora and braids down her shoulders, she went.
She went as a mother of children's children.
She went to seek refuge in the mammoth's arms.
****

One day, the pact would be known to the need-be kinfolk.
One day, the dirty dip net will overflow with frost-bitten whitefish.
One day, the polar bear will come to the child and give her seal eyes
for making medicine of twigs and ivory, belting chants of skeleton Inuit.
****

A driftwood mask let her be inside out.
The still poison of fish guts come up, gnarled
in layers of rabid willow ptarmigan,
inroads of dirt and dust makeshift the tides.
****

To repay *Samna* will be a lifetime of parkas.
Give the skins to the river's narrow nest lined with plumes
and dragonflies, humming to *igutchaq* bumblebee.
Inuit giants will laugh and the salmon will roast.

****

Then, she will take the shell lenses off,
let her goggles lie next to the granite rock,
pull her braided hair down in truffles of seaweed, and wear the parka.
This day is made of horned puffins and Eskimo soothsayers.

Tingivik Tatqiq: September Moon
Ukiaksraq: Early Fall Moon when
the birds fly south *Inukshuk*:
A scarecrow rock structure made
by piling up stones in order to
steer caribou in a certain direction.
Our time when bear, moose, and caribou
are hunted, then put away for winter.
Her/my many wounds close. Fish are
cleaned, dried like my eyelids with
alder wood splints she/I gather/s *Masu*
wild potatoes placed in sea oil.
Tinniks or bearberries purple
like her/my veins picked in
caribou fat. She is/I am a Scarecrow
mixed with Bear with pilot
bread like a wafer of eucharist
to control the herd.

Oil is a People   will she/I jump the edge?
She'll/I'll walk   with wrists sliced   by burdock
Her/my eyes   fixed and formed
like ironwood.   She/I watch/es a bulldozer drag

black peat the surface   land not broken,
only fragmented   like green   fused moss.

Eleven thousand years   is not enough
      to climb north   to the timberline.
         Not enough   to watch you
ash women out of breath,

while quickly   picking salmonberries.
     She'll/I'll walk   as if an arctic cat
        swallowed her/my air   then my blood.

She/I wait/s late   this summer to pick berries,
east of the crossing   where the slow   fire burns

the overlapping blades   and lungs, the mouths
of tall grass   into tufts and petal shrubs.

She/I smell/s the pungent lead,   gray smoke
from the shoreline   of the old village.

She/I hear/s cadaver ash   whispering
where your ceremonial house   once held
the winded songs   of gypsy moths.

Now   up in flames   blue oil burns

it fumes high   at her/my shoulder
as vapor gouges   earth into a different

form of wind.   Flames transfer   heat like hollow
         bones but differing like   a steel pipeline.

Four months ago   she/I drove the caribou

to the point into cold water. She/I follow/s you
looking past   the fog   but imagine
a night   when we collect smooth   ocean
pebbles   brought on white waves.

She/I see/s the pipeline   cracking, the Haul road
paved.   Oil dripping on the tundra   she/I fall/s asleep
as you are dancing with the dead. Your head adorned
with angel-white, loon feathers.
                    She/I can't stop the friction
of oil and gas   drilled   with a thin scale
         attached to fins.   Is she/am I going mad?
She/I use/s her/my teeth   to drill cold   but maybe she/I can
         work metal   tungsten   steel
into thick seaweed.   She/I fall/s deeper,   deeper to sleep.
She/I make/s an ice shelter (in case the cold doesn't work).

Warming

She and I make a bladder bag to draw water from the ice trench.
She/I chain stitch/es a skin dressed in oil to make a new pot of soup.
She/I sew/s a badger hair rough around the top of her/my *kamiks*
to make the steps windward, toward the limits of woman.
She/I eat/s club root and white clover to strengthen her/my silver
body to bear a child. She/I map/s, following 1 degree from the North
Star and 60 degrees from the end of the earth's axis on rotation
for *Ukpeagvik* she/I use/s a small arc of ice, cleaving into parts, reduced
to simple curves fitted with serrated edges of white flesh. She/I mold/s
to the fretted neck of frozen water into a deep urn, made like a rock shelter
or a cavern. She/I construct/s a hole on the surface of a glacier formed by melting particles
of roe and pan reservoir dust from a shelter for the ice worms. Because the earth is
molding, burning, laughing, and purging its crust.

Her/My Arctic

Corpse Whale

It comes back to the Inuit me:
images   in the mirror are closer   than they appear

on my kayak skin boat.   She/I was forged by sea salt
by snow   hammered   into iron ore   red herring.

While she's/I'm paddling   another floating corpse,
a spotted human pelt   a narwhal is passing
                a turquoise iceberg.
Of plucked   bones of ivory   with spiral blood   stained ribbons

reduced   to a single   tusk. She/I pass/es,   and keep/s paddling,
in a sea with gray   and choppy   scarlet walls of water.

Our carnage fuel oil   wicks in lighted igloos
on polar seaboard   next to washed up
empty   blue-green coke bottle   fishing floats,
floats   mark a thread   bare seine net   packed with arms

       of purple octopus   grabbing the rearview mirrors.
                She/I keep/s paddling.

Towing a nine-foot tusk   draggle   a blood trail,

gaff the glass and blink. The eyelids   shun risky   long-handed

Braille   rope: pacts.   Her/my eardrums playing   an
old throat song,
dry as sunspots.
       She/I keep/s paddling.

In a lidless cesarean section   of ozone layer   is a white giant
looks through   a tainted glass rope porthole

adopts young Inuit   like mottled jellyfish, suck
blood quantum   and raises underground   flags beneath Polaris Star.
        She/I keep/s paddling.

Her/my flouncing caribou   in dark moonlight are dodging   Bush laws.

Her/my Malamute   trots in Arctic circles
before the midnight   storm.
Her/my ringed seal barks   couplets of foreshadows   in an oval
tasting

room
with white columns and musty   yellowed law books.
She/I keep/s paddling.

Reaching the shore   of the Beaufort Sea landing the kayak

she/I witness/es in triple-thick   permafrost of sea   and land merging,
the Inuit skeletons are rising like brittle   driftwood ivory
as the Stellar Eagle   plummets and she/I try/ies pushing,

pushing, and shoving   the sinew back   into the threaded
            bones of the land.

The Weight of the Arch Distributes the Girth of the Other

If she/I maneuver/s   with the new moon—   her/my   shadow-shadow/s

shift   to the dark side,   hold   her/my distended
stomach/s   if she/I watch/es him   shape change in the
              morning hours   will the weight   of the arch shift?
         The adoption is final. The girl raven is beautiful and round.
                    Envisage the bestial nature of man,
              summon an innate mother's love for her new girl part raven.
As a hound pines   to be a wolf   a rosary prayer string

made of snowberry seeds severs her wrist.   See a small ray unlock   the namesake

in soft gleams of   light circumscribed   by dry root in   the other.
Killbear.
She/I=daughter=namesake=Killbear from Wainwright not far from Barrow=raven woman.

A Violin in Blue

Aubade

a black beetle runs across white stone,
intermezzo, allegro
spring water coda: passage.

Processional

A knotted pine
leaks sap. It hardens—
then falls.

Interlude

In Russia the time is thirty-seven
past the hour. Sixty miles east,
a day and thirty-seven minutes past the hour.

Antedate: Opus chime

Burning the coarsely ground myrrh,
surmise unspoiled
wafers of wheat.

Offertory: Rhapsody

Peeling, curling white birch bark,
our flax in linen skin,
a vat of saffron to bathe
bright, grace note in B.

Recessional: Absolute solo

Nuliavik Tatqiq: October
Moon when Caribou rut
Fall: *Ukiaksaug*
The western arctic caribou herd migrates
through the Noatak and Kobuk River Valleys
berry picking, fishing, and hunting, are
still going on around the region. Hunting
seals, walrus, and whale occur in the coastal
parts Inupiaq are sowing, carving, ice fishing,
making and mending nets.

For the Spirits-Who-Have-Not-Yet-Rounded-the-Bend

Iivaqsaat   *for my dear mothers*

> When an Inuk leaves a round home and enters into a square house he
> gets a headache and gets nervous.
>
> —Armand Tagoona, 1926, Inuktitut at Rankin Inlet
> on the coast of Hudson's Bay; ordained priest, 1960

I. Light

The seal talked to me with sharp eyes in my dream.
Altered, I was able to be with both of you mothers.
Light the seal oil lamp, elder women, as I draw thunder
from the sky at dusk. Water crests on the river sound like beams touching the surface or
a spark crystal in a whiteout. A flare falls on the edge of the ocean, I shudder at the black,
dry snow. Seldom have I thought of rapid growth in years, you both with heads of hair
like whalebone strings: white, and tenacious. I seldom listen to only one voice or, to only
those standing in a row in the night. They stand up as rays of sunstrokes, just when the
night turns to a gleam ripple on the glass water. Then, as the ligature of Inuit light flux and
flows like herds of walrus, passing along the coast, this is a seal hook of bear claws clipping
me to the northern tilt, pinning me to the cycle of night when the day slows, the wind
shifts to cloud, and the moon shadow grows to sun loops. It is then I answer the coal seal
eyes with throat song, standing on one strong foot in dance with white gloves.

II. Natural World Adoption

I learned to crack mussel shells, to collect moss on rocks, save strewn caribou hides across malleable tundra; how to stop my finger joints from cracking in frost, to dye my hair garnet to fit in, to feel earthquakes uprooting soapstone and jade, to count milliseconds by watching a brook run, to count cracks in an ice floe, to drink water from a horsetail reed. Now, my ball and sockets rub and roll the way hummocks bound and rivet the northern tip of the Rockies. I read books until my eyes chart points in words down 4000 miles in desert sounds. My tongue clipped to the brow antler, the words rubbing sealskin to make thunder, then lightning. I guide the harpoon-line hanging in the singing house with many blessed eggs for mothers, for children. I stitch you around my eyes, down my chin, though my altered states to remember it is you who guards me from long ice needles. Is it you, threading the singe on my sealskin, patching letters tied to ink blood. I am seeing only willful DNA tattooed to the snow knife for cutting ice blocks of chins, perhaps for a house, a shelter, a lean-to in a starved storm but, had I not prayed for this moment, this dissension into fish or birds, if what I wanted was to make it until the large stocks of dried musk oxen are gone. Then, I would choose sable day and flux night.

III. Man's Law

I think of that day 14,156 days ago, when in blackness we first shared eyes, domed eyes, in Anchorage, as the place on the old river, as the place where spiders braid, not where laws stay on one bank of the river. We are in the upside down world, where the sunless earth came into cold and then at once turned over to firelight. Yes, my home where black flint makes arrowheads, where slate makes knives for sharpening fingers on smooth, dark whetstones, each filed to a perfect 3 inches. One finger per hand to point like a ruler, to measure words on paper a-foot-at-a-time in concrete, paved increments in proxy's, in dusk and glare of another steel box. Mother, I was taken in dark dawn to drink from a whale-bone cup, to use a bird dart to catch willow ptarmigan and grouse, to smoke a pipe made of willow stick. I used a stone maul on my underground thoughts of you. I caught bees for you, placed them in a silent box to dry when you dance in grandfather's ceremonial house. Sometimes, I'd find myself naming my doll after you, practicing for when I learn to dry northern pike on alder poles, learn to break their necks below the head on the first bone of the spine, learn to slit their bellies of blood flesh like berry juice or boil their eyes in their head for soup. Every year or two, I prepare to sod my roof, so I can make do another winter. I make a hole in the ceiling for smoke and prayers to rise together in song. I remember cleaning smeared smelt off my hooks sharpening them to catch mirror-back salmon its fins spread, heading the opposite way, nosing up the river to spawn in eclipse water when the sun moves around the earth and all days are ebony backward.

IV. Flesh Tools

I ask you two old women, both I have always known,
please lower your eyes to the water crests, see the sun
stroke the surface and flick my scaly flesh. Watch in
the underbrush a herdsman corral caribou that stray
having lost many to the tundra clans or the cross.
But you, resting by a fish rack in the willow gorge
north of Lynx Lake, was it you using a fish wheel
to turn water spinning and now, years later, after eating
wafer bread you give me a drink from an ivory dipper?
Now, I lay in fields counting cotton grass; I see only one
of you walking toward me blurred, lighter than you were
in the past, less body with hollow bones, starving
like fossil ivory, like the ones I found petrified
in streambeds or in dry snowdrifts. I gauge stone
bladed grass measure to you as in a small abandoned
village to the world's full sod house. I cast a purple
flare in aurora when a mean low tide blows the heavy fog
inland around my body like a veil gathers the shore. And
you see me in a long parka, in *mukluks*, dancing in the
midnight sun not for law, or man, but for whale and blood.

V. Spirit World

In a feast from the messenger, I pray you ask for me in moon smoke, ask for the truth tracing the upright twirl of dark madness into white light; leaving cairns and effigies behind. In realms less traveled with bowheads, I will settle down to give you this tight bundle of charts and maps to find me not in unnatural shapes, but in bear grease, in your bowhead counting, along the sea, in body, in eucharist, in a seal effigy. Then, when the bones surface in late stages of calling, with coiled willow root around their wrists and ankles yes, I pray, then when the flare falls into ash, ash onto the shoal, and we at the end of the pier, mend and sow, waterproof seams of muskeg tundra to thank whale people for oxygen. After the border of flesh and church, after the old book is read, when ivory and scrimshaw are used with rib tools to create *Okvik* not Christianity, when the bell tones across the sound until then, I will wash ashore in a dazed whiteout, hide flesh to beach with my fore-claws hanging limply, my hooded golden eyes with concentric circles, lines on my chin, with a large backbone for my lungs, and a heart of spotted wings.

The Flying Snow Knife

after Inugpasugjuk

After: When Houses Were Alive, Technicians of the Sacred, 1969

One day in the village, a snow-knife rose up and out the sealskin flap portal in the ceiling and flew, traveling to the top of the ice cap. It was a bright day, and it is said the sun watched the knife cutting the stars, creating half-spirits-of-light. The knife had not yet reached the end of its flight when an *anaqtuk* shaman begged it to come back to him. It came back, hovering. The sun got upset with the *anaqtuk,* but the *anaqtuk* had no good-will amulet in exchange to the sun for the knife. So he gave him a hunter-Raven's dead body. The *anaqtuk* grabbed the ivory knife just in time. The moment the *anaqtuk* caught the knife, the sun eclipsed with the moon. Raven brings the light.

The Sun, Moon, and the Dead Raven

after Inugpasugjuk

When it became daylight after the eclipse, the Sun went back home with a new husband, the Raven, from visiting her brother, the Moon; the Sun gave the dead man life by warming him with her rays of red like the outer layers of willows. The Raven/man came alive, his body, severed into seven stars, became the dipper in the night skies. It is said hunters use an ivory bone dipper filled with water to pray with, for help during their hunts. They give a drink to the felled animals for their journey. For the animals are always grateful and return each season, giving their lives to the hunters. Now the Sun does not miss the snow knife, now she has a husband *Tulunigraq*.

Nippivik Tatqiq: November
Moon of the Setting Sun
Frozen Path to the Moon
Siqieiq: Sun
Tatqibiksuq: Moon Shines
On 16 mounds from 500 ad
She/I roam/s into *Piqniq*
In 2010 November a whiteout
Blizzard. Ice age hares,
And lemmings scatter.
The sun scorched her/my hair
And shoulders snow nectar
Mother, you know it's
Iced up in Barrow I know
Your igloo is sharing rose light
with me/her together.
She has/I have never known
you to be wearing pink roses
in your hair.
Carnivores: wolf, fox, lynx,
wolverine bear, stalk us.

Whalebone Wolf Hunters Dance

A *Senunetuk*: a whalebone wolf hunter ´
creates a whalebone arrow
in a Z pattern, he gently slides the sharp end
into walrus blubber, freezes the fat
whole, then places it in a trapline.
A black-tipped silver wolf eats the frosted *muktuk*.
Thawing in the stomach, the dart springs,
piercing the membrane lining.

> *Isibru*: a whalebone wolf slayer
> oblique holes for eyes in a wooden
> mask with a dancing gorget rises to the hunt.

Tonrat the Watchmaker Bestows His Wishes on Her/Me

May it happen   going   through the crawl space
into the snow light   may it blind   you like a warning
                  from the watchmaker.

                                            Ticking   tocking   socking.

May it happen   as your harsh voice rasps   in a whiteout
you awaken   the dead whispers
                  of rattle mittens.   Clicking. Clanking.

May it happen   like a stone   door opening

          as you murmur   with the old ones tongues
in the most   blessed time   as song   in the high forest.

May it happen   in stages   between an open   wound
          and a healed immortal.   May it happen   in due time

a white coyote barks   to the walrus   gut drum.   Rocking.

May it happen   in the stillness   of the night sea
          watching a ringed plover   fly with the wave
ripples   as you awaken   from sleep.   May it happen.
                                  Tocking   Ticking.

Tulunigraq
Something Like a Raven

Dances for *Qarrtsiluni*
to Change   the Steps Home

Under a salt white moon   *Tulunigraq* dances

to the braided night shade.   He toe hops   on blades

of sea grass   his feathers shine   like Acoma black on
black pottery   his beak   a locus of tool and song.

He sings into the purple morning   clicks and caws
in medicine words waits   waits   for something to break.

Qarrtsiluni sitting   in silence   where all things
and all beings reach   back into time   before iron
and oil.

Like his cousin Crow,   Raven Man clicks and caws
in verse time   told tomorrow   461 years ago   and today.

In the same moment   of stillness   over the Tongass sledge

at high day   Raven lights   a whale oil lamp   by the sun's rays.

It is said Raven   flickers the way   for the Inupiaq
he sings click,
click, caw because   rarely is there any,   one place to call home.

She Sang to Me Once at a Place for Hunting Owls

Utkiavik

I wade through the nesting ground, fitted like a fingerprint. You say it's a place of speckled day owls with golden eyes. You and I traveling together, following the caribou at the entrance of *Quunquq* River, we see caves in old sod houses which belonged to reindeer herders. Our dogs start barking, whining. We follow the whale-rib steps up to the ridge, leave tobacco. We keep hiking up the mountains where there live many Dall sheep, we set camp. I dream of a snow bird with pearlescent plumes, a horntail, and a spiked crown. She brought me a lens to use in the echo chamber. When we come upon *Okpikrauq* River, I hear her song vibrate off the cliffs:

> *People have as their names, their rivers, their rivers.*

In Wainwright's Musk Oil Spermary

for OW

A charwoman   enveloped in dark   heavy colored smoke   returns
her/me Wainwright to breed.   When she/I send/s   me back
she/I afflict/s   parching

heated rocks   as an offering   to the spirits.   Soaked in tallow   a red-
throated wren and a lemming   with four hoofed toes   hang on her
shoulder eating at her/me

water fleas and louse.   With a single breath blowing she/I glean/s
charcoal rot and the fire   burns higher.   A wretched doll
dances on a

string its   shadows mark the walls   of the *tupik*.   She/I touch/es the
blue trade marbles on the ground.   They seem hard cold   smooth.
She/I

throw/s them like marbles they roll. Crouching she/I see/s three human heads
carved   from walrus   teeth   fastened on the charwoman's
       marmot belt. She/I sit/s down   to the flood scoured
ground   she/I see/s a butchered   black brant   suspended
on red willow sticks   turns   slowly over the fire-pit.
She/I envisage/s a feast   like the one in *Nunamiut*   *Kaktovik* or the one
of bloodroot   and river otter. It was if her/my   impulse/s impulse/s
impulse/s   of the throat

        to swallow   chokes. The burnt gut   salivates in the back
of mouth.

Her/my reaction/s   to the burns created   more saliva.saliva.
saliva.   As she/I crest/s Wainwright on the last hill   where she/I flee/s
the spawn lair

the charwoman forbids   her/me to go. With her hands   she gives me an
empty glass bottle to collect   feathers from the golden plover.
                And there she/I stand/s   rummaging   through lice
and frothy blood.   I realize now   she's/I'm
the donor   the giver of life   the mother   the twin sister
the earth and the   Raven.

Her/My Seabird Sinnatkquq Dream

for SB

She/I awake/s breathing and whispering,
twice born, twice born
on the brim of an ice casket,
in the hindmost of the devil's mob,
at the forefront of the angel's winged flight.
She/I enchant/s a song from the bottom of the seas,
her/my smile bare like a hair comb
with rows of bone teeth.
Her/my eyes blink in wisplike feathers,
she/I sing/s, *Drift along, drift along,*
plenty of time to know the song.
She/I keep/s humming to lift herself/myself up,
her/my whispering stops. She/I raise/s up
from her/my knees.
Stunned at first, stunned with a fist up,
her/my eyes affixed on the clock,
as it goes around and around.
The moonlight on a curved path
reflects on the wall, she/I shine/s like a ring
moving from place to place, a moon dance,
here and there, circling the mirrored globe.
Startled by a whistle I run to the window,
she/I look/s out the bubble,
she/I see/s his enlarged outline
come to vision through the fog haze.
His white face with a black streak,
orange-yellow nose and mouth,
his eyelids lined in flame,
he shakes my head, a powder white

mist glows slowly by. As it lifts
see him take flight with tufted horns,
and darted wings, he glides an inch
above the ocean grass. He sings to her/me
with cousins and they whistle back,
a stealth sea cormorant, brants,
horned puffins, murres, and great
auklets. The sea spray stings her/my cheeks
in realization, her/my head sunk, shriveled
below her/my sternum, neck and thorax
beating freeborn. They sing her/me to the ledge,
a nesting ground, alcoves of feathers
preening—the image pulsating—
in her/my temples, wrists, hips,
and ankles. She/I drift/s along the sea
walking the cliffs thinking,
birds are the vessels—they fly but there
is prevalence in death and a means
to reseed—on earth. She/I hear/s the dry trills
I commit her/my soul, the sea birds bind
her/me to the grave.

On the steppes they tell her/me only
when the wind breath blows.
She/I call/s *Sila* to bring glacial drifts,
he's the driving force of the sea
weather which salts her/my spirit,
opens her/my gilded doors, widens
her/my dreamscape down to the bottom.
Serpent Samna points and shoots
her/my non-zero numbers, she/I respell/s
and modifies the far side of the poles.
Create a passage in transmitted
light then a red flash following,
a red flash. The seabirds dive in
angles into the sea—she/I follow/s as if
knowing the course down into the ocean.
Focused and let her/my body emit light,
we follow the schools of hooligan
to *Samna*'s catacomb. She/I purge/s my breath

soul she/I spew/s forth to *Aselu* all her/my energy,
to the sun. They give her/me a painted
and feathered mask, a wooden gorget,
on my hands they put rattle shell mittens.
She/I start/s to sing from my throat from a deep
place inside me. The songs know
change and movements of the earth,
underworld sea, and blue heavens.
The song comes from the keepers
of coffins and breathe-life, runs on sunlight,
using only what it needs, fits form
and function, recycles everything,
rewards cooperation, rests on diversity,
curbs excess from within, and taps
the powers of the universe, she/I said: *dust born,*
dust death—he said: *it's ash, ash all of it.*

Ukiuk: Winter *Siqinrilaq Tatqiq*: December
Moon with no sun *Ukpeagvik*: Barrow
Tuluqraq: Raven
A high place for viewing; a root of a point
2 feet from the left, 71 degrees north,
Gateway to the Arctic
in the center of the earth a gingko tree
is planted. A hole drilled in rocks
penetrates where the flesh is easily
separated where her/my roots grow.
Her/my cadaver sings an old honor slow low.
For she/I want/s confession with a full
wafer and a drop of wine.

Chain Link Fence at the End of Tin White Life

A steel wire   wraps around   her/my hinged wings as she/I try/ies
to wake. A tailless rodent: matted   filthy and vermin
gnaws   at the four-membered rings. He attaches me
to this ashcan.   The chains clank   like metal studs— shaking her/me
            to be ear-minded.
She/I rip/s   where the junction   of two bones   on her/my ankles
rub raw like a rust wheel   link by link.   Link by kink.
She/I swivel/s around, on her/my blind   feet to hear   the segment of
speech   by the devil.   It churns and echoes   into the sinkhole,
        plunking down.   She's/I'm pushed by a head of horns   outward
as the vesper   bell tones   and she/I make/s   her/my way
into   tin white
life.
                            bell   tones   bell
tones   bell
tones

A Ricochet Harpoon Thrown Through Time Space

You   be mean and slavish her/me   to your invisible
surges of electrocution   which weakens   the swag
            as she/I walk/s.   You gave her/me away to strangers.

She is/I am encircled   by doors with red alarms   roosting
            waiting to open   to flex lace veils   of blanched thought

like she/I would   succumb to night. But she/I belong/s to them now.   She is/I am

bound   to thrive even in a desert   of sand. Will you not
diffuse or possess her/my tact or sit   poised on her/my glacier   watching it
            become a reflecting pool?   She/I tamp/s her/my pipe

savor the sun's   energy and learn   to ricochet   her/my harpoon
time dilation: slowing down   23 thousand mph   stretching
out of time.

A Cigarette Among the Dead

Now   as the days length 11 hours and 50 minutes
     its stretch   of gnawing snow   bares her/my *inua*.

And from   the macabre marring   and mania which hems
     her/me in   and cleaves   her/my wretched blue   heart she/I
stare/s   into the night.

Dazed by the lantern   she/ I detach/es from   my carcass.
     She/I indulge/s in a cigarette   among the dead, my hand

shakes as   she/I reach/es the ashtray   to flick. She/I know/s
     they won't give her/me back
     satisfied by the loll of backfire   and noxious

coy of smoke   which eludes   her/my eyes swirling
into blue.   She/I take/s solace in disarray   and ravish

     in a trysting   place fitted for my digressions
ripening and raw. Her/my mind   sanguine and far-off

     a solemn growth   in matter to lessen   the scorch.
The air breathes   and delves into   my bloodless

bones each   decomposing, cast down   in the dark
cast down   in the light   to gladden
the shades.

An Anatkuq's Marionette of Death

I. Musk Moth Larva

He hooks the grapnel, *aablak*: on the depression between her/my shoulder blades—
the gouged ache of tethered, threaded muscles tear. Where her/my every breath
compresses, the *Anatkuq* inches out my/her madness through his hands. She/I
contemplate/s his work in dolls. She/I watch/es, seated high above on a shelf, over
the table, above the fire: she/I remember/s him as he scraped, soaked, and dried
the tiny dolls, knowing she/I was one of them.
Once, on the third of the month, on the shelf in a stilled pose, he grabbed
her/me in a tweaked burst—played with her/me, and drove out of her/my spine a hair-
winged caddis fly, then threw her/me to the ice in one swift motion, returning to his table
to pin the wings on cardboard, labeling the insect in pencil script:

musk moth ink larvae.

II. Mock Casket

Her/my topaz eyes crash the window shut, the glow fades.
She/I feel/s out of place, out of land, out of past; perched

on the sill, a fruit-flesh-fly exits in a high stagger,
scuttles across the room, burrows in her/my hairless ear.

His buzz, silence fused in amber, remains for the cracking-
open to meet the air, free born, not fixed in puzzlement.

Her/my thoughts add to the cold because dark ice keeps heat,
traps bugs. She/I feel/s a breakdown down: her/my feet burn,

stung by weeds; her/my fingers decrepit, popping. She/I blood-spit teeth,
travel/s on foot through niches and layers of space, her/my *inua* tangled

in this night. When morning comes, she/I succumb/s to the bare, blue ice, raise
her/my hands to my eyes with her/my legs crimped in a mock casket.

III. Twin Brothers Lay Her/Me in Sulfur Death

black spirit/light spirit

she/I clamor/s damp   and hard in her/my bed,

brothers of glow   and shade   do/es she/I stand/s

as voiced song?   Or in an image of your

twixt—likeness of snow   vapor rising?

You, brothers/sisters   in scorn,
       sweep around me   like a flock of pica.

She is/ I am entrenched   as a dead spindle
 achieving   only hunger   not willed peace.

You suffocate her/me   with your curved teeth,
       sink   in her/my chest   as a coarse   nettle burns
her/my hairless   thin skin.   No angel or demon

in heated death   can rescind her/my   naked tail.

You bite on the 7th cervical in her/my neck;

you prod at the nerve   cord in her/my back

your heavy   splayfoot   death pierces her/my
spinal column   she/I arch/es her/my back it tweaks.

The sulfur-stench permeates her/me
the white forest   creates fear and crucifix dust—

enough to melt   the polestars   enough to fillet
sturgeon for eggs   bringing near   nil-of-existence.

Eskimo Eskimo Eskimo Eskimo Eskimo.
Never   Never   Never   Never   Never   Never

IV. She/I Run/s in Night Bloom Flowers

She/I lick/s pollen with her/my bristled tongue off night-
       blooming flowers   watch old crows   in a downpour

see four-limbed   scavengers on   dagger claws
gaff   their teeth into dry   chalky bone.

Twenty snowless   tiered burials on   stilted graves
loam across the field.   Why does a monarch caribou

kill the   breeding bulls   of the herd and   leave antlers?
Above an open grave   an imperial moth glints by.

In a dream   she/I remember/s   at *Kalaallit Nunaat, Greenland,*
     a moose ripped   by the canine   teeth of black
wolves.

Her/my scream   shrill and piercing   casts signals
conjures echoes
                    echoes   between   bats and bugs.

In those echoes   are Inuit mastodons   ground squirrel
 ice bears   mastodons   ice bears
musk oxen   stellar eagles   blue jays and ravens.
                                                                    And ravens

ravens.

Loose Inuit Glossary

aablak: the depression between the shoulder blades

aanaga: my mother–grandmother

aapaga: my father–grandfather

aapiyaba: brother

aarnaruie suliuqpa: savannah sparrow

afipchabaa: resurrects him

agaayuvifmufniaqtufa: I'm on my way to church

agaviksiuvika tatqiq: moon for beginning whaling and finding ptarmigan

anatkuq: a shaman; person endowed with the power to do much good or bad

aqavirvik tatqiq: August moon when birds molt

atiguluq: dress

Birnirk: prehistoric Inuit civilization of north coast Alaska 500–900 AD

Ibeivik: June birth time; moon when animals give birth

igutchaq: bumblebee

imieauraq: prowler and shaman

inua: animals with nonhuman existence but have no immortal soul

inuk: person

inukshuk: scarecrow

inyukuksaivik tatqiq: July moon when the bird raise their young

isibru: a whalebone wolf slayer

izrasugruk tatqiq: February; coldest moon; literally ice moon time

kabloona: Inuktitut old term for white man; new term qallunaag

Kaktovik: town in central north slope

Kalaallit Nunat: Greenland

kamiks: my boots

kusruqaqtubvik: literally moon of a higher sun

kuukpik: river off the Colville river, upriver from Nuiqsat

Masu: underground potato or bulblike plant

mukluk: any boot of ugruk soles (not an Inupiaq word)

mukluk/maktak: the edible skin of whales about an inch thick directly under the harder outer tarplike skin covering

nipiruq: sunset

Nippivik tatqiq: November moon of the setting sun; frozen path to the moon

Nuliavik tatqiq: moon when caribou rut

Nunamiut: Alaska's inland Eskimos

Okpikrauq: owl river in north slope; my family names river

Okvik: old Bering Sea people 150 BCE–700 AD

Okvik Madonna: in central Asian arts and arctic regions, a sculpture statuette

Paniqsiqsiqsiivik: March moon hanging seals; bleaching caribou skin

Pigniq: shooting station

Ptuquqsiibayuk: stag beetle

Qarrtisiluni: sitting together in darkness waiting for something to burst

Qupixbubrauq: edible ice worm

Qurraquaraq: killdeer

Qusrimmak: wild rhubarb

Quunquq: north slope river

Samna: also known as Serpent Sedna; it means the one down there, not visible

Sauniq: bones

Senunetuk: a whalebone wolf hunter

Sikuibvik: thaw

sila: the breath soul in the wind; also known as Silap inua or Silla to mana or ether, the primary component of everything that exists, method or locomotion for any movement or change. Sila is believed to control everything that goes on in one's life.

sinnaktuq/sinnatkquq: dream

Siqieiq: sun

siqiniq: sun

siqinrilaq tatqiq: December

siqinyasaq tatqiq/January: season begins with the moon of the coming sun

suvluravik tatqiq: May moon when rivers flow

tatqibiksuq: moon shines

tatqiq: moon

tatqiq kusrugaqtubvik: coldest moon; ice moon time; moon of a higher sun

tingivik tatqiq: September moon

tinniks: bearberries

Tonrat: a watchmaker

tulugaq: raven

tupik: coastal tipi made of hides

tuungaq: devil

ugruk: bearded seal

Ukiak: winter

Ukiaksaug: fall

Ukiaksrauq: early fall

Ukpeagvik: Barrow (town)

Ukpik: owl

Ulu: woman's knife

Umiliak: whale hunting captain (in this case my older brother Eddie Rexford)

Upinagaq: summer

Upinagasrak: spring

Uqaluktuat: Barrow, Alaska

Uqaqtaa: god, prophet, apostle, literally: god's speaker

Utkiavik: a place for hunting owls

Utqiagvik: Point Barrow

Acknowledgments

My deepest gratitude for this book's beginning, which was composed at The Institute of American Indian Arts, Port Townsend Writer's Program; Naropa University for the middle; and for its completion at Soul Mountain Retreat and Stonecoast College at the University of Southern Maine.

My earnest acknowledgments go to *Red Ink Magazine, To Topos: Ahani, Many Mountains Moving, Future Earth, Washington Square, Effigies: An Anthology of New Indigenous Writing, Sing: Poetry from the Indigenous Americas,* and *Drunken Boat,* where versions of these poems have appeared.

I wish also to express my appreciation to my family: The Creator, Nellie Nanuq Okpik O'Neill, Vera Williams, Cathy Tagnak Rexford, Mary Sage, Allison Worden, Eddie Rexford, Tracey Miller, Brandy Lee and Stormy; and to my extended family: Rachel Craig, Sadie Brower Neakok, Donald Stearns, Margaret Stearns, Edward White, Dennis Stearns, Paul and Anne Burger, Ty, Travis, Yvonne, and Cyril Burger; and also for the leadership and scholarship of Corwin Clairemont and Linda King, Arthur Sze, Jon Davis, Marilyn Nelson, James Thomas Stevens, Allison Adelle Hedge Coke, Heather Cahoon, Jody Perez, Orlando White, Layli LongSoldier, Sherwin Bitsui, Jennifer Foerster, S. G. Frazier, Britta Andersson, and my darling husband, Myron Burger—without their support and friendship this book would not have been possible.

About the Author

dg nanouk okpik is an Alaskan Native, Inupiat—Inuit, from the arctic slope. Her family resides in Barrow, Alaska. In 2003, okpik received the Truman Capote Literary Trust Award. She graduated with an AFA in 2004 and a BFA in Creative Writing with honors in 2005 from the Institute of American Indian Arts in Santa Fe, New Mexico. She went on to get her MFA in Creative Writing at Stonecoast College at the University of Southern Maine in Portland in January 2010. *Effigies*, her first chapbook, was released in April 2009. okpik has been published in *Red Ink Magazine*, New York University's *Washington Square*, and in the Oregon Literary Council's *Ahani Indigenous Writers Anthology*. Her work has also appeared in *Many Mountains Moving Journal*, *Poet Lore*, and *American Poet: Journal of the Academy of American Poets* recently emerging poet award by Arthur Sze. Most recently her work appears in the anthology, *Sing: Poetry from the Indigenous Americas*, edited by Allison Adelle Hedge Coke and published by the University of Arizona Press. dg nanouk okpik currently works at the Santa Fe Indian School in Santa Fe, New Mexico.